# FACILITY MANAGEMENT BRINGS WHAT BENEFITS



JOHN LOK

# Contents

*Preface* *v*

*Prologue* *vii*

1. Human Behavioral Network Job Brings Social Economic Benefits 1
2. Robots Take Our Jobs Behavioral And Economy Influences 5
3. Intellectual Human Economic Behaviors 10
4. Facility Management Brings What Advantages To Influence Behaviors 14

# Preface

Introduction

Behavioral economy is one useful and fun social subject. Behavioral economists usually research how and why human behaviors may influence economy growth or recession, or how and why economy environment changing factor may influence human behavior changes.

Facility management strategy may bring what advantages to influence organizational behavior? How it may help the improve to employees performance and bring positive emotion to consumer behavior? **Whether do any organizations need facility management department? What function of benefits will bring when the organization sets up one facility management department? If the organization lacked one facility management department, what the disadvantage it will bring to influence the organization's operation? Does it has relationship between raising efficiency or improving performance and facility management department?**

In my this book, I shall attempt to explain how andy why ecommerce may be one kind network human job. Also, I shall indicate reasons to explain why human network behavior may bring direct or indirect influences to economy growth or recession in our global societies in macro and micro economy view. I shall indicate cases to explain any possible human social activities may bring direct or indirect influences to cause our social economic growth or recession in consequency in possible. I hope that my readers can feel more understanding whether what real meaning of behavioral economy is the relationship between our behaviors and our economy.

# Prologue

Contents

Introduction p.3

Chapter 1

Human Behavioral network job brings social
economic benefits

What does human network job mean p.4-8

Why human network job behavior may influence economy p.8-12

Chapter 2

Robots take our jobs behavioral and economy influences

Robot job behavior brings economy influences p.13-29

Chapter 3

Intellectual human economic behaviors

What does intellectual human economic behaviors
mean ? p.30-40

**Chapter 4**

**Facility management brings what advantages to influence behaviors**

**Facility management functions**

**Facility management brings what benefits**

**Facility management brings what benefits to organizations p.41-45**

**Facility management brings what benefits to economy**

**Facility management can reduce maintenance service expenditure p.46-49**

**Facility management role in organization p.50-54**

**How (FM) space moving management can bring valued add to organizations p.55-60**

**Reference**

***Predictive the choosing right data asset and (FM) analytics***

***solutions to boost public***
***transportation service quality***
***The relationship between facility***
***management and productive***
***efficiency p.61-64***
**The relationship between facility**
**management and consumer**
**behavior**
**Facility management brings what benefits to entertainment theme parks p.65-69**
**Facility management brings what advantages to theatres**

# ONE

# HUMAN BEHAVIORAL NETWORK JOB BRINGS SOCIAL ECONOMIC BENEFITS

What does human network job mean ? Why may human network job be popular? Why human network job behavior may influence economy ?

Nowadays internet is popular to use. We can apply internet to find data , search any new things, even earn money. Why does internet

may become huma network job source. For example, e-publish may be one kind of new human network job. Any authors may apply internet

channel to help them to sell electronic or paper books from e-publisher web store. They may apply facebook, you tub etc. any online

channel to promote themselves new books to let new readers to know whether when they may buy themselves favourable new topic books to read

from electronic publisher web store.

Thus, future electronic publisher industry may help any authors to build internet network platform to help them to sell and promote

ot advertise their any one new electronic or paper book topic to let global any one reader to choose to buy their any new topic books from electronic publisher web store easily and conveniently. However, it implies that electronic network platform author may be one kind of future new human network job in our societies.

How electronic network platform author job may bring economy benefit in macro economy view? A person can have few friends, contacts and still be very influential if these few

friends and contacts are themselves highly influential, e.g. one author must not need to know any one reader in global society. When they like to choose any electronic books from electronic internet network platform. They may become the author's any one topic book buyer, when they feel the author's any one topic book is fun and attract they make decision to buth the strange author whose the topic book from electronic book publisher's platform web store conventiently in short time. Although, they are strangers, they do not know themselves , but the reader can understand what it way that made Google from writing platofrm to create new creative mind and typing network job method to replace traditional hand writing book method for global authors. It will be one kind of new human network writing job.

Hence, global any one reader can apply an innovative search engine , such as google.com to find whether whom author personal new topic books are value to read from internet.

Then, the electroniuc publisher's web store may be new book store platform sale network to help the author to sell many electronic or paper books from electronic network platform in short time. So, internet may be future new network plaform to help global any one author to create network writing job absolutely. Furthermore, internet may be popular social media

to help any one author to build goold relationship between his/her readers. It is one kind of new network, human network job. New authors do not need to buy many paper books to prepare to put in any one book shop warehouse. Their every book can print on demand to reduce out of book stock in any one book shop. They may choose to sell either electronic books or paper books both from any one book publisher web store. So, electronic network platform may be one kind of good writing channel to help human authors to create income and it can also

help authors to bring new creative mind and new topic fun content books to let readers to know and buy to read from electronic publisher network platform.

Why does human behavior may be one kind of new human network job to bring global economic advantages. ALthough, it may be free income or without inocme, but the person does the network behavior, his/her behavior may be bring advantages to influence many other people's health. For this case, when a worker in a coffee shop in an airport gets a vaccination aganinst the flu, it does not only helps him or her stay healthy, but also helps the many travellers who might otherwise have been inflected if that workers caught the flu.

So, the externality , the result implies the vaccination of even a part of a community conveys benefits to the whole community. For example, governments pay special attention

to the vaccinations of school children, teachers, health mothers, and the elderly, categories of people particularly susceptible not only to catching, but also to transmitting a disease.

It is not accidential that governments are heavily involved with vaccination . When there are externalities, free market, fail to persuade individual incentives with society's

their the worker's decision of whether to get a vaccine ends up attracting whether other people get sick. The workers might not fully take all these other people's potential suffering into account when making her or his vaccination decision.

As Stanford University does many suggestions, understand this and tries to help them make the right decisions and so providers free flu vaccines for its staff and students.

Small pockets of unvaccinated individuals can allow a disease to gain a spread more widely well-being. For example, parent weighing the costs and benefits of a vaccine for their child is not always thinking of the consequences of that vaccination to other people. THese are markets in which subsidizing or regulating behavior can make everyone better off. Because the reason for requiring that a child be vaccinated before enrolling in school is not just to protect that child, because each child's vaccination affects others via potential contagions.

# TWO

# Robots take our jobs behavioral and economy influences

Robot job behavior brings economy influences

If one day robots can replace human to do simple, even complex jobs. They will bring what influences to our global societial economy.The popular economic refrain declares that the

global middle class is dying and robots will soon take our jobs, e.g. shopping center customer service jobs, library service jobs, cinema ticket sale jobs, restaurant kitchen cooker jobs,

even, bus drivers, taxi drivers etc. public transport driving jobs, accountant, doctors etc. professional jobs. Whether it is beautiful or petty matter if our future societies have many human jobs can be replaced to do from robots. Businessman must may reduce to employ employees and reduce to pay salary or wage, when robots can be replaced to do their employees tasks. But, societies must bring unemployement rate rises , due to societies will have many people loss jobs when their employers choose to buy robots to serve their clients or do any office tasks or customer service or cleaning etc. tasks.

In micro economy view, employers may save money in long term, but in macro economy view, it will cause unemployment ratio rises , even crime rate rises when there are many people lose

jobs in societies. These models of doom, though, fail to account for the hundreds of businesses riding the waves of change in their industries when robots may be invented to replace human to do many simple , even complex tasks in our future societies.

WE may image that one small factory needs to manufacture fishes canes to sell to supermarket, the small , cheaper stuff and higher margin parts of the fishes manufacture industry. Before, this factory needs to employe many human factory workers need to help every fresh customer makeing the perfect fishing gear, designed for performance, durability, and cost in order to achieve to manufacture every fish cane in whole fished processing manufacturing stages. Every worker needs to spend about 15 to twenty minutes to finish every fish cane , till to delivery to any supermarket to sell. If this fish canes manufacturing factory can apply manufacturing robots to help them to finish any one working tasks , every robot can only spend five minutes to finish whole fresh fish cane manufacturing process. Thus, every robot can help this factory save 10 to 15 minutes time to finsh every fish cane manufacturing process. IN fact, time is money, because when every robot can help this factory to reduce 10 to 15 minutes time to compare human worker. Then, this factory can finish about 20 fish canes in one hour if it can use robot to help it to manufacture fish canes. Otherwise, if this factory still use human workers to help it to manufacture fish canes, then it can finsh about 3 to 4 fish canes in one hour. SO, the manufacturing efficiency ensures that robots must help this fish manufacturing factory to raise fish canes number more than human workers. So, in robotic behavioral economy view, manufacturing robots must help this fish canes manufacturing factory to raise fish canes manufacturing number and deliver increasing number to supermarkets to prepare to sell every day. Robots can help this fish canes manufacturing factory bring manufacturing time saving, rising manufacturing efficiency, improving performance and reducing wages expenditure long time advantages in micro economy view. However, manufacturing robots can also bring disadvanages to society, e.g. increasing unemployment ratio, increasing crime rate,

this factory workers will lose jobs and income, they need earn social welfare from government and increasing government finance pressure in short time, even long time in macro economic view.

Stanford University graduate program in economics, Scott lecturer explained that "in demand and supply economic theory for robots supply and demand case, robots supply number increasing may influence human workers demand number decrease. It sometimes calls " the efficient frontier".

No specific human beings were mentioned in any of economics classes. As robots supply and demand in market case, They ( robots) may be purely theoretical " agents" who reached to the most reasonable sale prices in order to persuade any one businessman buyer to make manufacturing robot buying decision whether robots can help him / her to bring how much saving time , saving money, saving cost, improving performance, efficiency economic benefit before he/she plans to reduce workers number when he/she decides to apply robots to replace human workers in his/her factory or office or any service department, e.g. cinema ticket sale service, shopping center customer service, shopping center cleaning , supermarket customer service etc. service or sale tasks. When robots can replace human to do any one of these tasks in any organizations. So, robots may be human worker agents who reached to prices the way robots would react to a software

command. There was nothing that explained why some people thrived and others did n't or why truly brilliant, hardworking people could fail when much lazier folks succeeded." Having been admitted to the Stanford University graduate program in economics, Scott lecturer hoped to get his answers there.

How robots influence our future social changing? Using the right technology can be a boon to your business in this economy. For internet example, it is easier than ever to find well-matched customers

all around the world, to stay in contact with them, and to more quickly design the products they want. If you focus solely on being cutting -edge, though you risk letting the technology

take over what should be very robust relationships with your customers , employees, and colleagues. IN nowaddays society, technoligical advances and cutomation, personal

relationships in business are more crucial than ever. I mean that robots can not replace human to serve clients to let them to feel more comfortable and passion more easily. For shoe shop case example, if the shoe shop apply one robot to serve its clients to replace human shoe salesperson to serve its shoe customers. Robots ensure that they can not persuade every shoe potential buyer to make shoe buying decision more easily when robots need to contact every shoe potential buyer. The reason is simple, because robots can not touch any one shoe buyer individual emotion very easier.

If the shoe buyer needs the robots to help him/her to choose any right shoe styles when he/she can not feel himself / herself can make the most right shoe style choice decision. The robots can not replace human shoe salesperson to make shoe style choice judgement more easily. They must need longer time to analyze whether which shoe style may be the most suitable to the shoe buyer. Otherwise,human shoe salesperson may attempt to make the most right shoe style choice decision to help any one shoe buyer to chooce the most right style shoe because he/she owns shoe style sale experience, shoe style knowledge, the most important reason is that they can feel every shoe customer individual emotion to touch whether he/she will feel comfortable or happy when they attempt to help every shoe customer to seek the most right shoe style in every shoe customer whole shoe searching processing. Othwerwise, serving robots are only one machine, they can not touch or feel every shoe customer individual emotion whether he/she feel comfortable or unhappy or happy when they need to contact them in whole shoe searching processing. Hence, I believe that some tasks robots can not repalce human staff to do very easily. Otherwise, robots may bring disadvanatges to let any one businessman to loss his/her customers, due to robots can not touch every customer

emotion to compare human staff in service tasks more easily. Robots serving customer behaviors may cause money lose and customers number lose to the shop in micro economic view.

# THREE

# INTELLECTUAL HUMAN ECONOMIC BEHAVIORS

What does intellectual human economic behaviors mean ? I believe that when we choose or decide to do intellectual behaviors, then our societies will be influenced to bring economic growth in consequence.I shall attempt to indicate pollution case to explain how and why eithet our intellectual or foolish behaviors may bring economic growth or recession in consequence as below:

On one hand, for air pollution social case aspect example, if we only consider to buy cars to drive for working aimr or holiday leisure aim. Then, our societies air will be polluted. Our health will be influenced to bad. Our car driving behaviors may cause global environment air pollution serously. In long tiem, global air pollution will bring our bodies health to be bad. Although, ourselves car driving behaviors may bring our driving travelling leisure enjoyment and comfortable feeling in short time, also we so not need to pay public transport fare often, but we need to compensate ourselves health economic intangible loss due to air pollution , when cars number increases, dirty air will cause ouselves health to become bad.

In the result, we will need to pay more medical expenditure when we are old age, due to ourselves bodies will become bad, due to we breathe global dirty air every day, due to ourselves cars pollute air in long time, e.g. 10 to 20 years, even 30 more without limited air pollution environment. So, driving cars behavior may be one kind of human foolish behavior and our foolish behavior may bring ourselves future long time medical expenditure absolutely.

One the other hand, water pollution social aspect, if we often keep much rubblish to pollute sea, oil exploration porcessing pollute ocean , ships gas pollute ocaen, then fishes will eat polluted food and drive dirty water, due to global ocean is polluted.

In fact, because human only to conside how to buy boats to carry on leisure enjoyment activities, or catch cruises to travel on the sea. Also, oil manufacturers only consider researching anywhere to find new oil exploration places to manufacture oil product, when their oil exploration processes pollute ocarn . Consequently, global fishes drink polluted warer or eat polluted food. They will have poison. SO, human will have high chance to eat poison polluted fishes, due to fishes are poison or are polluted.

So, human is doing foolish activities, we only hope to find oil exploration places to pollute ocean or we only spend money to buy ticket to catch ships to travel anywhere in global ocean. All of these human foolish behaviors will bring pollution to global ocean. On consequently, we will need to compensate to eat polluted or dirty or poision fishes, ourselves bodies health will be bad. In long time, we need have high chance to pay medical expenditure when we are old. So, pollution case may be one good example to explain how and why human foolish behavior may influence ourselves future need to compensate serious medical loss.

All of these human foolish behavior will bring pollution to global ocean. On consequently, we will need to compensate to eat polluted or dirty or poison fished , ourselves bodies health will be bad. In long time, we will have high chance to pay medical expenditure, when we are old. So, pollution case may be one good example to explain how and why human ourselves intellectual or foolish behaviors may influence future long time economic loss or economic growth or recession in micro and micro economic view.

On another water pollution aspect hand, if we often keep rubbish to sea, oil exploration processing pollutes ocean and ships' gas pollute ocean, then fishes will eat polluted food and drink dirty water, due to fishes will eat polluted food and drink dirty sea water because the global ocean is polluted seriously.

In fact, because human only consider how to buy boats to carry on any leisure water activities, or catches cruises to travel on the sea. Also, oil manufacturers only consider any where to find oil exploratin places to manufacture oil products from ocean, when their pol exploration processes can plooute ocean. Consequently, global fishes drink polluted water or eat direty food. They will have poison. So, human will have high chance to eat poison fishes.

Otherwise, such as pollutin case, it can infuence inflation or deflation. Consequently, the reason indicates supply and demand theory. If air pollution is serious, then we will consider health issue, global cars demand number may be influenced to reduce, when global cars number demand will reduce, global car prices and supply number will need to change to fall down in order to attract or persuade global car consumers choose to make car purchase decision.

Hence, global car manufacture number and car price will be influenced to reduce, due to global air pollution issue. Consequently, deflation will occur because when the country citizen usually does not spend much extra saving money to buy car expensive goods. Money value will be low. Otherwise, if global cair pollution is not serious, human considers to buy cars to enjoy driving leisure lives. So, global car demand is influenced to increase , also global car price will also influenced to increase.

Consequently, gobal human will choose to buy cars to drive. Due to we accept to spend extra saving to buy expensive car goods. Car sale price and supply may be influenced to rise up. Money value is influenced to reduce. Inflation may be influenced, due to global car consumers number increases, we would not have extra money to spend easily. Car expensive goods expenditure influences our spending habit to avoid to make car purchase decision more easily. So, human intellectual or foolish activities may bring inflation or deflation consequency in possible indirectly in macro economic view.

On conclusion, above pollution case explain that how and why human intellectual or foolish economic behaviors may bring inflation or deflation consequency as wll as economic growth or recession consequency as well as any goods demand and supply increasing or decreasing consequency. It implies that human behavior may have indirect relationship to influence any goods demand and supply number to either increase or decrease result as well as any goods price will be influenced to increase or decrease in micro and macro economic view.

# FOUR

# FACILITY MANAGEMENT BRINGS WHAT ADVANTAGES TO INFLUENCE BEHAVIORS

**Facility management functions**

**Why do many organizations begin to feel facility management importance? What are the real functions that when one organization can attempt to achieve facility management strategy? The main functions of facility management may include. For example, when sale manager is directly responsible for managing the performance of salespeople, facility management seems that it can not help any salespeople to increase sale number, they have no direct relationship, but in fact, any salespeople must need to stay to sell any products in the shop. SO, the shop's facility environment may have indirect**

relationship to influence customers purchase emotion, when they enter the shop. If the shop's facility is more attractive, it may let customers to feel comfortable to stay long time in the shop.

So, facility management influences people, processes, the building and technology to be improved better in order to achieve good job performance or sale performance both in possible. This serves many broader goals, improving efficiency, and productivity and creating a positive workplace culture, coordinating desk arrangements, managing employees, facilitating moves and spaces utilization, handling emergency planning benefits to any organizations.

Hence, the facility management function to service aspect, they may include submitting a work order request rapidly ( raising efficiency) , when the shop can be designed to have more space for service staffs to contact customers , it aims to let they feel comfortable to stay in the shop, reserving space and visitors and handling emergency action planning more easily. When the shop customer service counters have effective enquiry place facility environment for customers and customer service staffs in order to let they can feel comfortable to stay to enquire and answer in the shop's service counters in long time.

ON physical building improvement aspect, effective facility management many provide repair, maintenance, and building improvement, workplace , cleaning , on-and-off site property management , e.g. improving security places to avoid theft occurrence easily. Moreover, more importance is needed for facility managers to understand and use technology, workplace management system aggregate data, which drives crucial decisions about how to run the business and shape the workplace, a modern facility management building, offices , factories , shops even living houses in order to raise smart building concept comfortable feeling to let house owners, shops staffs and customers factories workers, office staffs to feel smart facility management system lay let them to feel comfortable when they are working or living in the smart building. So, smart facility

**management system may bring these functions: Researching IOT devices based on data collection needs, integrating IOT devies into everyday facilities processes, determining the cost, ROI and using aggregated data to better understand the workplace.**

**Hence, in one smart building, facility management system can collect and analyze data from networked technologies to get insights about the workplace. This fuels better decision-making on how to optimize the work environment for the people using it. For example, all smart office technology relies on data collection , access control system supports safety, when automation technological streamlines processes. And when these is a data component to any networked device or software, the true benefit of most technology is in its function. So, future smart offices , houses, factories etc. building will be needed to apply facility management technology to let any one feels comfortable when they need to use the building smart office or house or factory automatic turn off light facility when the office facility management system can help all the building all offices to turn off the light or central air condition automatically in order to save power or reduce energy waste in any office inside working environment any time when the facility management smart system ensure that none any one is staying in the building any offices.**

**Hence, facility management ought bring these benefits to any business office users or house living users, they may include tha complete management and maintenance of the buildings, people and assets of the business, it enables a more cost-effective working process within the business, it improves the efficiency of the business, e.g. raising workers productivities when they need to stay long time in the factory to manufacture any products, if they feel the factory environment is more comfortable and safe to let them to work, their emotion may be influenced to feel more happy to work, even raising the product manufacturing number more efficiently, it improves the efficiency of the business, it helps to manage health and safety requirements in accordance with**

industry requirement, helping a workplace run at maximum efficiency, e.g. cost reduces, space optimization , creating a comfortable feeling in a better workplace, outsourcing facility management service may brings better service delivery, more variety snf flexibility, today's employees and tenants expect more then just clean restrooms and adequate lighting to create and enhance great company cultures.

So, FM provides and manages a variety , it supports services in order to organize all the organization's functions more efficiently. It focuses on the integration of primary activities on both strategic and operational levels. Moreover, facilities management can be defined as the tools and services that support the functionality, safety and sustainability. For outsourcing facility management advantage., it may involve turning over the complete management and decision making authority of an operation to somebody outside organization. It may help businesses to maximize returns on investment and establish long term competitive advantage in the marketplace.

Hence, the types of facility management may include: cleaning, hardware inspection and maintenance, transportation, security service, fire safety. However, there are some differences between facilities management function and property management function. In general, facility management and office management are concerned with the people using the space, when property management concerned with the space itself only, e.g. the physical building shell and rented offices etc. buildings.

Facility management brings what benefits

Facility management brings what benefits to organization

Can facility management bring social benefits? What benefits do facility management bring to our societies? What are social responsibilities to facility management? Why do our societies need facility management services? I shall attempt to explain as below:

IN fact, ay organizations will need facilities management services, because it can bring continuous development benefits on

**economy, environment and society aspects, e.g. minimising waste to landfill form the organization, when the organization has effective facility management service, increasing supply chain opportunities, when the organization can apply facility management skill to arrange how to let warehouse or store space can keep goods to put on corrective positions and more space to put their goods in warehouse. So goods can be transported to move more easily when the warehouse can have effective transportation to different countries more efficiently in short delivering time as well as when global warehouses can have effective facility management service to be arranged how to store their goods in warehouses efficiently in order to bring rapid transportation benefits between the country and another country. It is significant " rapid goods transportation benefit" to any organizations. For Amazon example, it needs to manage different goods to keep to its different countries warehouses in order to transport goods to fly to different countries customers' homes every day by air plane rapidly every day. If Amazon can have effective warehouse facility management strategy to manage how its different kinds of goods to be putted on its shelves in its different countries warehouses. Then, it's logistic workers won't need spend much time to seek any goods on shelves in order to deliver their goods to fly to another country in short time efficiently. So, Amazon warehouses facilities management service can help its organization to provide efficient delivering service.**

**How can facility managers satisfy the needs of customer when such needs changing so frequently to their organizations? Organizational justify theory indicates that where managers do not have resources available to meet employee demands. The procedures used to divide what resources are available may be used to achieve satisfaction. How can facility management satisfy needs of customers when both these needs and environments in which they are operating change as frequently? How to match unpredictable space demand with supply? How to manage refurishment of out dated facilities, dealing with the competing**

space and service demand of different departments.

So, it brings this question: How can facility and accommodation management groups appease their customers in the intermediate term? SO, it seems that facility management can raise our social organizational justice benefits, such as improving service performance and raising customer satisfactory feeling for the organization's efficient service performance.

IN fact, efficient facility management strategy may help our social any organizations to earn these benefits. They may include: Influencing employees' perceptions fair procedural fairness in our social organizations, the provision of timely feedback and effective communication of the basis for decisions. So, effective facility management may help global organizational managers to know hoe to allocate new space that has become available to let employees to feel enjoyment to work in order to raise efficiencies or improve productivities. It will create any country's GDP growth when the organization can implement effective facility management strategy. Hence facility management can bring benefits to improving customer satisfactions, improving productivities and raising efficiencies. Then, our social organizations will have more social benefits, when GDP growth is caused by facility management service improvement to any global organizations.

Brochner (2003) pints out the reality that innovation in jointly FM brings benefits to organizations , developing goods and associated services in manufacturing is starting to surface, when the connection between facility design and management is still weak, IN organizations, FM can meet organizational business need more appropriately, attract customers more are easier to manage and control and operated more cost effectively, respond better to occupant needs.

After all, design has an effect on sales efficiency, staff, profit , capital investment, and maintenance cost( Ransley and lngram , 2001). These factors are the concern of facility management as much as they relate to the organization's core business success.

Therefore, managing FM requirements during design is necessary for an organization to achieve its goals after occupancy a newly build facility.

For airport facility management case example, an effective management of the facility , aimed at successfully satisfying both the airport ownership and the passengers ( air plane travellers) customers, should be based on agreement, network and strategic allience with FM functions from other airports, they can apply outsourcing FM strategy to provide facility management service during travellers are staying in their airports, they can feel enjoyment in airport environment, then their shopping desire and again visiting the country's airport desire will be influenced to raise, when the country's airport can provide comfortable FM airport facility to let them to feel. Hence, FM can raise customer service perofrmance with firm's objective and service processes, drive performance improvement and increase client satisfaction, such as airport travelling places whehter how FM may influence travellers to stay how long time in the country's airport. It means that when the airport is more attraction, e.g. design is attration. Then , the airport can persuaded travellers to stay long time in the airport. Consequently, their shopping chance will increase in the airport.

Facility management brings what benefits to economy

The economic benefits of FM organizational design . Evidence is growing that FM may help buildings provide financial rewards for building owners, operators and occupants. FM buildings typically have lower annual costs for energy, water, maintenance / repair, reconfiguring space because of changing needs, and other operating expenses. These reduced costs do not have to some at the expense of higher first costs, Through FM design and innovative use of high quality of materials and equipment, the first cost of FM building can be the same as or lower than that of a traditional building.

Moreover, some sustainable design features have higher first cost, but the payback period for the incremental investment often

**is short and the lifecycle cost typically lower than the cost of more traditional buildings. In additional to direct cost savings, FM buildings can provide owner and society benefits, for example, FM building features can promote better health, comfort, well being and productivity of buildings, occupants , which can reduce levels of absenteeism and increase productivities. Moreover, FM buildings can also often owners economic benefits form lower risks, longer building lifetimes, improved ability to attract new employees, when they feel office environment or warehouse , shop working environment are more comfortable to let they feel, when they are staying in these FM workplaces, reduced expenses for dealing with complaints, and increasing asset value.**

**Overall, FM buildings also offer society as a whole economic benefits, such as reduced cost form air pollution , damage, avoiding landfills, wastewater treatment plant, power plants and distribution lies. So, low first cost and later repair / maintenance expense reducing or avoiding. Consequently, above of these will be FM building's long time economic benefits, social benefits and organizational benefits to the building owner, its clients and our societies.**

**Facility management can reduce maintenance service expenditure**

**Facility management provides a variety of non core operations and maintenance services to support any organizations' operation. For logistic organization example, it is possible to provide effective maintenance service to warehouse in order to reduce warehouse facilities to be damaged to bring to spend to buy any new equipment facilities expenditure. So, when the logistic company's warehouse facilities can be maintain to be the best quality. Then, they can be used these warehouses' machines facilities again. Their performance can assist workers to manufacture any products to keep the most efficiently an raising the best production performance in whole manufacturing process. Then, this logistic company's facility management department can bring to avoid purchase any new machine**

**facilities expenditure spending. One to these warehouses' production machine facilities are kept in the best production performance environment eve in long term production need.**

**The logistic industry's facility management department can create cost savings and efficiency of the warehouse's workplaces. It's machines facilities ( production machines) are dealt with the maintenance management of the physical assets maintenance service. FM ( facilities management) has been being applied to industrial facilities in logistic and warehouse industry long term as well as maintenance plays a significant role to ensure the full service and the warehousing system, including both building components and equipment in warehouse.**

**Maintenance service is needed to bring a certain level of availability and reliability of a warehouse facilities system and its components and its ability perform to a standard level of quality. So , it seems that logistic industry's warehouse asset cost reducing. It depends on whether it has one facility management department to provide maintenance service to itself warehouse workplace's production machine facilities and warehouse building itself in order to let workers t feel the manufacturing machines can bring good manufacturing performance to assist them to produce any products in one safe warehouse workplace environment. Hence, the performance measurement of warehouse maintenance issue will be valued to be consider to every warehouse manager and facility manager in logistic industry.**

**In logistic industry, (FM) works at two level on the one hand, it provides a safe and efficient working environment, which is essential to influence warehouse workers whether how they perform to do their manufacturing tasks or logistic goods delivery tasks in warehouse. When they feel the warehouse is safe environment to work. They will not need to consider anywhere has risk to cause they die by accident in warehouse. Hence, they can concentrate on doing their every tasks . On the other hand, it can involve strategic issues, such as property ( warehouse workplace and management, strategy property decision and**

warehouse facility, e.g. manufacturing machine, facility maintenance and checking planning and maintenance planning development.

However, reducing the operating expense issue will be the main aim when the logistic company feels that it has need to set up one in-house facility management department to carry on any maintenance service for its warehouses' any workplace property and manufacturing machines facilities. So, when the logistic company decides to implement one facility management department, it needs to ensure its facility management department can bring the minimum level of keeping manufacturing performance and efficiency to its warehouses' any manufacturing machines and warehouses' property to avoid to be damaged in short term, such as loss of business due to failure in service, provision of project to customer satisfaction, provision of safe environment, effective utilisation of workplace space, e.g. warehouse effectiveness and communication between the workers and the logistic managers in the warehouse workplace , due to the warehouse's space is not enough maintenance service reliability to the logistic company's warehouse, responsiveness of the warehouse's worker individual negative emotion problem, due to his/she often feels need to work in one unsafe warehouse working environment. Hence, it seems that poor or unsafe warehouse working environment can influence workers feel negative emotion to work to bring low efficiency ( inefficiency) or under productive performance in warehouse. It has relationship to influence they to bring psychological negative emotion feeling to work when the organization lacks one effective warehouse management repairing service to be provided to the warehouse's facilities and properties' maintenance needs in order to avoid ineffective measurement and misleading of performance.

Hence, the logistic company's facilities management department often needs to be reviewed whether its maintenance service level is passed to achieve the lowest repair ( maintenance) service standard to its warehouse itself property and

**manufacturing machine or warehouse delivery tool facilities or warehouse lamps' light whether is enough to let workers to see anything clearly to avoid accident occurrence or see anything to work clearly or the warehouse space areas are enough to let they can have enough space to walk or communicate to their team supervisors or deliver any goods more easily in the short distance between the worker's sending goods location and the delivering goods destination in order to avoid because the lacking enough space to cause the accident occurrence , due to the space is not enough to let they deliver their goods to any locations in warehouse.**

**Hence, it seems logistic company's (FM) department can contribute to the organization's mission, such as avoiding warehouse accident occurrence, inefficiency, inadequancy and unavailability of the facility for future needs when the warehouse lacks enough space areas to bring poor performance of facility and dangerous warehouse itself property in warehouse, e.g. safe and reliable operations of material handling equipment and maintenance of warehouse facilities, grounds, security system, utilities, plumbing, heating , enough lighting system, air conditioning, warming heater, fire protection, security system alarm etc. facilities in warehouse.**

**Hence, it seems that if the logistic company expected to reduce to spend lot of excessive manufacturing machine purchase expenditure, losing of workers' life or bring workplace accidents , due to poor warehouse workplace environment, even bringing lawsuit compensation claim loss , due to the worker individual accident or death is caused from the poor warehouse facilities, or bring negative emotion to let the workers feel they are working in unsafe warehouse workplace environment. Then, it ought choose to set up on facility management department in order to provide enough maintenance service to its warehouse to avoid these non essential expenditure causing , due to these poor warehouse facilities factors.**

**Hence any logistic company ought choose to set up one itself in -house facility management department, it be better than outsourcing its all facilities service to one facility management ( maintenance service provider) to help it to deal any kinds of maintenance service in warehouse. Because it is long term maintenance need to its warehouse's any machines and warehouse itself properties. If it chose to find one outsourcing facility management maintenance service provider to replace its in-house facility management department to deal all related facilities maintenance tasks in warehouse. Then, it is possible that it needs to pay long time facilities maintenance service fee to its outsourcing facility management maintenance service provider more than itself facility management maintenance service provision department.**

**In conclusion, to decide whether the company ought need or not need facilities maintenance service or either set up in-house facility management department or outsource one facility management maintenance service provider. It depends on whether its organization has how many facilities are used in its workplace, how many staffs are working the workplace, how much size of its workplace, its workplace is office or warehouse or factory, how long time of its facilities' useful time etc. factors , then it can decide whether it needs or does not need one facility maintenance service department or outsource facility maintenance service provider to help it to deal any facilities management problem in its organization.**

**Facility management role in organization**

**When one company feels that it has need facility management service. It can choose to set up either in-house facility management department or seek one outsourcing facility management service provider to help it to arrange any facility management service need. However, this facility management role is only one for the organization. It concerns this question: What facility management maintenance function can bring the**

**benfits to the organization?**

**It can define that all services required for the management of building and real estate to maintain and increase their value, the means of providing maintenance support, project management and user management during the building life cycle, the integration of multi-disciplinary activities within the built environment and the mangement of their impact upon people and the workplace. In traditional, (FM) services may include building fabric maintenance, decoratin and refurbishment, plant, plumbing and drainage maintenance, air conditioning maintenance, lift and escalator maintenance , fire safety alarm and fire fighting system maintenance, minor project management. All these are hard services. Otherwise, cleaning , security, handyman services, waste disposal, recycling, pes control, grounds maintenance, internal plants. All tese are soft services. Additional services, might also include: pace planning, things moving management, business risk assessment, business continuity planning, benchmarking, space management, facilities contract outsourcing service arrangement, information systems, telephony, travel booking facility utility management, meeting room arrangement services, catering services, vehicle fleet management, printing service, postal services, archiving , concierge services, reception services, health and safety advice, environmental management.**

**All of these services will be every organiztion's in-house facility soft or hard services needs. So, it explains why some large organizations feel need one effective facility management department to help them to arrange how to implement facility serivices efficiently in order to achieve cost reducing, raising efficiency and performance improvemen aims because one effective facility management control system can influence employee individual productive effort to be raised or reduced indirectly.**

**However, (FM) can be selected either setting up one in-house (FM) department or outsourcing its services to one facility**

mangement service provider to help the organizatin to solve any kinds of facilities maintance service problems. One on-house (FM) department is a team, it needs employees to deliver all (FM) services. Some specialist services are needed to be outsourced, when the service is on expertise in the company. The no expertise services will be outsourced to simple service contracts, e.g. lift and escalator (FM) department will have direct labour, but it can outsource some specialist to help it to do some complect facilities management service. So, the team leader can of can manage whose team staffs, such as maintenance technicians run low risk operations . Otherwise, the outsourcing facility management service provider needs to help it to operate high risk operations or maintenance vital plant facility management service. Anyway, it can set up in-house (FM) department to arrange specialist direct labour and outsourced (FM) services to more than one facility management service providers to do different kinds of (FM) services. One of these outsourcing (FM) service provider, who can arrange sub-contractors to assist it to finish any (FM) services of it's outsourcing (FM) services are more complex to compare the other sub-contractors ( third parties).

- What is a facility manager's role to provide quality service to satisfy its user needs?

We need to know how quality can be defined in facility management and why it should be defined by the customer? How facility managers can find out customer (user) needs? What are the difficulties in finding out users' needs and in delivering quality services? Whether improving quality always means requiring higher cost?

In general, facility manager's major responsibilities may include these major functional areas: longer range and annual facility planning, facility financial forecasting, real estate acquisiton and/or disposal, work specification, installation and space management, architectural and engineering planning and

**design, new construction and/or renovation, maintenance and operations management, maintenance and operation management, telecommunications integration, security and general administrative services. When the facility manager had implemented any one of these FM services for those user. How does he/she provide excellent (FM) service quality ot let whose users to feel satisfactory?**

**In fact, quality issues can not be considered without customer-oriented perspective service quality involves a comparision of expectation with performance. (FM) service quality is a measure of how well to service level delivered matches customer expectation. So, these issues are (FM) service user's general measurement level requirement. The (FM) manager needs to achieve these the minimum performance measurement level to satisfy whose (FM) user's needs.**

**However, (FM) service quality has three characteristics: Intangibility, heterogeneity, inseparability. But in fact, (FM) service delivered may be through tangible physical aspects, e.g. factory plant workplace building, machine equipment maintenance, intangible (FM) services, e.g. managing space moving in plant to let staffs to work, managing outsourcing cleaners to clean factory equipment. However, all (FM) service performance often varies, due to the behavior of service personnel. Hence, a well developed job specification and training can help to improve the consistence of services of (FM). Any (FM) productin and consumption of many services may are inseparable and they are ususally interactions between the (FM) client and the contact person from the service provider.**

**Hence, it seems that service quality is considered as hard to evaluate. In (FM) service quality, it includes physical quality and interactive non-physical service quality. Physical quality is tangibles: The appearance of the physical facilities, equipment, personnel and communication materials. Non-physical services quality means reliability: The ability to perform the promised service dependably and accurately; responsiveness means the**

**willingness to help customers and provide promopt service to let user to feel; assurance mans the competence of the system in its credibility in providing a courteous and secure service and empathy means the approachability, ease of access and effort taken to understand customers' needs.**

**Hence, a good performance of (FM) manager , he/she ought satisfy the user's tangible and non-tangible both service quality needs. I recommend that he/she can attempt to predict what are the (FM) customer expects in each (FM) service needs. Then, it can make decision what aspect(s) will be the (FM) users major (FM) service need and what aspect(S) won't be the (FM) users major (FM) service need. Then, he/she can make more accurate decision to arrange time, human resource , cost spending amount arrangement whether when it ought concentrate on finishing the (FM) major service tasks as well as whether how he/she ought finish the major (FM) service tasks to be more easily, e.g. how to arrange staffs number to finish, how many the minimum staffs number is needed to be arrange the major (FM) service tasks, time arrangement is important factor, because it can influence whether he/she ought finish the major (FM) service tasks today or tomorrow or later in order to have enough time to finish other non-major (FM) service tasks. Instead of time management, staff number arrangement is also important factor , if he/she arrangeed the excessive staffs number to do the (FM) major services tasks, then it is possible that it will have shortage of staffs number to finish the non-major (FM) service tasks on the day. So, avoiding either majoe or non-major (FM) services can not finish on the day. The (FM) manager needs to predict when the major (FM) services and the non-major (FM) services which are necessary to be finished in order to have enough time and staffs to assist him/her to finish every day major and non-major (FM) servie effectively. Then, the achievement of his/her (FM) major and non-major tangible and non-tangible services , it will have more chance to be performed efficiently by his/her managed staffs.**

**In conclusion, in any organizations , (FM) manager needs have good predictable effort to evaluate whether when his/her managed team need to finish the major and/or non-major (FM) tasks as well as whether how he/she ought arrange the accurate time and staff number to finish any major and/or non-major (FM) service tasks on the day. Then, his/her leading of (FM) service team can be managed to work more efficiently in order to satisfy her/his (FM) service user's needs.**

**How (FM) space moving management can bring valued add to organizations**

**There are interesting questions: How (FM) can bring value-add to avoid loss or earn more profit to the organization? Can it influence employees to raise performance and improve efficiency ? Some organizations' (FM) service need which is necessary in order to let employees can raise productivity.**

**It is based on these assumptions: I assume the organizations have completely either outsourced or in-house their (FM) facility management departments will gain more effect on added value than they have no (FM) function as well as organizations have a strong coordination with the (FM) department will gain more added value than organizations with a weak coordination. Organizations in the profit aim can gain more added value than organizations in the not for profit aim sectors.**

**In fact, any organization is difficult to confirm it has relationship between improving performance, raising efficiency and owning (FM) function in its organization. (FM) could have to do with the attraction of easy but incomplete indicators of efficiency rather than the necessarily and less direct measures if the effectiveness and the relevance of space moving useful management, e.g. whether building has the enough space to let employees to move to work easy in order to raise efficiency, whether the building has excessive furniture and equipment number and they are putted on wrong places to be caused employees move difficulty in the building in order to influence productive performance.**

However, how to arrange space moving management to equipment, e.g. copying machines, faxes, productive machines, they are putted on the locations where have enough space to let employees to move to another locations. For example, the building floor has more than 50 employees, but its space is not enough to let these 50 employees to move to any locations to let them to feel easily often. Then, it is posible to cause they feel nervous pressure and they can feel difficult to work , when they are working in a small office space or factory space or warehouse space. Then, the consequence will be under-predictive efficiency or poor performance to any one of these 50 employees in this office or factory or warehouse.

" Facility management is responsible for coordinating all efforts related to planning, designing, and managing buildings and their systems, equipment, and furniture to enhance. The organizations abilty to compete successfully in a rapidly changing world." ( F.Becker)

The author explains equipment, workplace internal space designing, furniture space putting location arrangement will have possible to influence employee individual productive performance or efficiency to be raised or reduced in the workplace. Hence, it seems that, in the value chain (FM) belongs to the activity part of the firm. To make the facilities cooperation with each office or factory or warehouse using space moving facility management. Facility space moving management must be linked strategically, tactically and operationally to other support activity to add value to the organization's office or factory or warehouse space moving management arrangement more effectively.

Thus, how to arrangement space moving management issue it will have possible to influence the organization's employee individual productive performance and efficiency in whose workplace. It seems that (FM) space moving management arrangement have indirect relationship to influence the organization's employee individual performance and efficiency

**, due to they need often to work in the workplace, if they feel moving difficulty , or excessive equipment , furniture number is putting into the small office, factory or warehouse locations, or they feel the office or factory or warehouse has excessive ( a lot of) staffs number to work in the small space of office or factory or warehouse. Then, they can not concentrate nervous on finishing every tasks in possible. In long term, their efficiencies will be poor or inefficiencies or their performance won't be improved or causing poort performance in possible.**

**Instead of the not enough space moving and excessive staffs number factor, it will bring another question: Can enough information systems equipment cause a more efficient and improved performance to the organization staffs in the workplace?**

**I assume that the office has 100 employees and it has only ten copying machines. So it means that ten employees use one copying machine. Hence, it brings this question: Is it enough to provide only ten copying machines to average ten employees to use? It depends on other factors, e.g. whether any one of these 100 employees needs to print how many documents per day , whether the five copying machines' locations are far away to separate different locations or they are stored in one printing room in the office, whether the day has how many staffs are absent, whether the day has how many printing machine(s) is/ are broken to need to be repaired. Hence, these unpredictable external environment factors will influence whether the five copying machines number is enough to let these 100 employees to use in the office every day. Hence, facility manager ought need to spend to observe average their copying behaviors every day in order to make data record. Many employees need to use copy machines to print documents, average how many document's page number, they need to print, how much average time spending to print their documents, average how many staff absent number on the day. Even, if the all five copying machines are stored in the printing room, calculating the staffs number whether how many staffs need more than five**

**minutes to walk to the printing room to print their documents many staffs need to spend five minute to walk to the printing room, and they have other urgent tasks to wait to finish. It is possible to influence their efficiency, due to they often need to spend more than five minutes to walk to the printing room to print documents. If there are many staffs need to often to print documents, but their printing task will have many time, e.g. 20 separate printing tasks. Then, they need to spend at least ( 20x5 ) 100 minutes to spend time to walk to the printing room to print their documents. It must influence that they should not finish the other urgent tasks on the day. If there are many staffs to spend much time to walk to the printing room in the least 20 separate printing time or more on that day. All the facility manager needs to evaluate whether all the five copy machines are stored in the printing room whether it is the best location decision or they ought need be separated to put on different office locations in their workplaces, even he/she ought need to evaluate whether it is enough copying machines number, when the office has only 5 copying machines. He/she ought need to buy more copying machines number to satisfy any one of these 100 employee individual copyiing task need.**

**In conclusion, effective office or factory or warehouse space moving facility management will be one part task of (FM) function. If the office or factory or warehouse can have accurate equipment, machine , furniture number to avoid excessive or shortage number problem to cause employees often feel moving difficult problem in their workplace when they need to move to another location to work in office or warehouse or factory as well as whether the staff needs often spend time to wait the another employee to use the copying machine to print whose document or fax machine to deliver whose document. Then, it is not that fax or printing machines number is not enough to provide the employees to use in the office or warehouse or factory workplace.**

**Hence, (FM) includes space moving facility management to equipment , machines, furniture number as well as choosing**

**anywhere is(are) the suitable location (s) arrangement to putting or storing these facilities in workplace as well as decision of the staff number and the workplace area size whether it has excessive staffs number to cause these staffs need to work in the small area size of office or warehouse or factory workplace. So, the organization ought need to decide whether it needs to reduce the office's staffs number to let them to work in another more suitable locations in another workplace. Hence, all these facilities space moving management and staffs and workplace size issues will be (FM) manager's consideration issues, because these external environment factors will influence employee individual efficiency and performance to be ppor to cause low valued to its organization in long term in possible .**

**Reference**

**Becker, F. (1990). " Facility management : a cutting edge field?" property management 8 (2): 25-28.**

***Predictive the choosing right data asset and (FM) analytics solutions to boost public transportation service quality***

**Can gather the choosing right data public transportation service station facilities asset and analytics, it can give recommendation to help any organizatin to boost service quality? (FM) analytics data can be applied to public transportation service industry to be supported how and why the train, train, ferry , ship, air plane, underground train public transportation tools' time arrival and leaving information notice board and automated ticket paying machines facilities are putting on or stored any where locations in order to boost passengers to feel their facilities locations are convenient to let them to buy tickets and see the arrival and leaving time for the next public transportation tool from the information notice electronic board machine. So, it seems that these public transportation tools' station facilities locations can influence passengers to feel the public transportation service company how to consider to its passenger's**

buying ticket needs and next public transporation tool's arrival and leaving time information needs in order to boost its passenges use service quality and let them to feel better service reliable performance in any train, tram, ferry , ship, underground tram, airplane stations.

As these public transportation service organizations need to learn data analytics represent an opportunity for its ticket paying machine equipment facilities as well as the next transportation tool arrival and leaving time information notice board electronic equipment facilities anywhere the locations are the most suitable to put on or store these equipment to let passengers to walk to the ticket paying machines to buy the ticket to catch the train, tram, underground train, ferry, airplane, taxt, ship more easily. So, they do not need to spend more time to find these facilities locations and spend more time to queue to wait to buy ticket to catch the public transportation tool in stations conveniently. Instead of where is the seeking ticket paying machine location, where is the next public transportation tool arrival and leaving information notice time , these both issues will be any public transportion tool's passenger's main needs.

Hence, how to spend time to seek where the next public transportation tool's arrival and leaving time information electronic notice machine location and where the ticket paying machine location , these both factors will influence any passengers' positive or negative emotion causing. For example, if the passenger feels diffcult to find the ticket paying machine in the large area size train station or /and he/she feels difficult to find the train time arrival and leaving information to let him/her to know when the next train will arrive the station. Due to he/she feels difficult to find the train ticket paying machine, he/she needs to spend much time to find any one tickeet paying machine in the train station. Then, it will influence him/her to choose another public transportation tool to replace the train public transportation tool, e.g. he/she can choose to catch tram, underground train, taxi, bus, ferry, taxi, ship to replace train. So,

**it seems ticket paying machine and time arrival and leaving information notice electronic equipment 's location putting or stored choice will be one factor to influence the passenger to choose another kind of public transportation tool to replace train at the moment. When, he/she feels that he/she arrives the destination in the most short time. Then, the public transportation service organization (FM) manager has responsibility to evaluate whether there are enough ticket paying machines number to let passengers do not need to spend more time to queue to buy tickets to catch the public transporation tool in short time as well as there are enough time arrival and leaving for next transportation tool to let passengers to know. It will be their concerning issues when they arrive the public transportation service tool's station.**

**Hence, predictive passenger individual walking behavior can help the public transportation service organization to choose whether where are the most convenient and attractive locations to let the ticket paying machines and the arrival and leaving time information electronic board machines to be putted on or stored in the suitable station positions in order to let many passengers can find these essential facilities in stations very easily. So, gathering data concerns passenger walking behavior in the public transporation service any stations, which can help the facility manager to make more accurate evaluation to attempt to predict whether where the locations are common places to let passengers to choose to walk daily or where the locations are not common places to let passenger to choose not to walk daily in general. Then, he/she can apply these data of different locations in the stations to evaluate whether anywhere they will have many passengers to choose to walk or whether anywhere they won't have many passengers to choose to walk in order to make more accurate decision whether anywhere are the most suitable locations to let the ticket paying machines and the time arrival and leaving information electronic board equipment to be putter on or stored in order to let them to feel it is so easier to let them to find.**

**Anyway, calculating each station's passenger number per day issue is important to predict whether where , there are many passengers choose to walk or where, there are not many passengers choose to walk in these different public transportation service stations in order to evaluate whether where the stations' different ought put on paying ticket machines or time arrival and leaving information electronic boards in order to let they feel very easy to buy tickets and seeing the next arrival and leaving time information for the kind of public transportation service tool conveniently in the different stations. Moreover, if the station has no enough ticket paying machines number to be supplied to let passengers need to spend more than ten minute time to wait to buy ticket to catch the kind of public transportation service tool in every queue every day. Then it will cause them to choose another kind of public transportation tool to catch go to working place or entertainment place to replace it to on that day. Then, it will cause these passengers who often do not like to queue in the kind of public transportation service tool's any stations, who will not choose to go to anywhere of this kind of public transportation service tool's any stations again. Hence, in long term this kind of public tranportation service tool will lose many passengers. Thus, calculating each station's busy time of passengers number , which can predict when it is the busy time and it can make more accurate decision whether the station has need to increase enough ticket paying machines number in order to bring enough supply number to satisfy passengers' ticket purchase need in the busy time.**

**In conclusion, gathering above all stations' public transportation service equipment facilities number, storing positions datas and every station's passenger walking behavior datas, they are necessary to any public transportation tool service industry, because these equipments' number and storing locations will influence them to make decisions to choose another kind of public transportation tool to replace it's transportation service if they often feel difficult to find these facilities in its**

**different stations. Thus, it is part of task to facility manager's responsibility if the public transportation service organization expects it won't lose many passengers , due to these external environment factor influence and it also implies cheap ticket price does not guarantee the passengers will choose to catch this kind of public tranportation service tool to go to anywhere.**

***The relationship between facility management and productive efficiency***

**It is one interesting question: Can facility management function bring benefits to raise productive efficiency to organizations? I shall indicate some cases to attempt to explain this possible occurrence chance as below:**

- **Facility management benefit to office workplace**

**In private organizations, when the firm has facility management department, whether it can bring efficient administration to influence clerks to work efficiently in office, e.g. reducing administrative time or shortern time to work in administrative processes, in order to achieve minimizing clerk number labor cost. How to design office facilities to let office staffs to feel comfortable to work and reducing their pressure to work. It seems that office working environment will influence office staff individual performance. If the office workin environment could improve efficiency and creativity of services to satisfy office workers' comfortable working environment needs. It will reduce every administration manager's working pressuse when he/she needs often to find methods to attempt to encourage whose administrative clerks to avoid to waste working time to do some non-major administration tasks.**

**Hence, how to design or allocate or arrange office any facilities' stored locations or whether how many equipment number is the enough to store in the locations, which will influence office employees' working attitude in order to raise or reduce their**

administration tasks efficiency indirectly, e.g. the office is clean or dirty, whether office receiption has enough information telephone switchboard operation facilities, whether every clerk's table has enough computers number to supply to every to use, whether internet speed is fast or slow in order to let any employees can send and receive email to communicate or download any document from internet in short time, whether data processing and computer system maintenance service supply is enough to be repaired to employees' computers immediately when their computers are broken to wait repaire, whether website editing facilties operation whether is enough to link to office every staffs in order to let any office staffs can apply internet to do their tasks conveniently in short time.

Hence, all of these general office equipment facilities whether they are enough supplied and their stored positions anywhere are the suitable to assist any clerks to work conveniently, they will influence every office employee's administrative and productive efficiency indirectly as well as all faxs, copying machines, computers, whether internet linking maintenance service time is short or long to prepare to any office employees to use conveniently any time, these different issues will also influence every employee individual efficiency in office. Hence, it concludes that office working environment, facilities supply number, facilities maintenance service and facilities location storing both factors will influence employee individual administrative productive efficieny in office.

- facility management benefits to service working environment

Can effective facility management improve service working environment to raise employee individual work performance? It is a concern about the quality of service to its customer question. The term" standards and goals" are often used to measure staff individual service performance whether he/she can serve to customers to let them to feel this staff's service performance or

**attitude is good or bad.**

**Is the service workplace working environment facilities enough, it will influence customer service staff individual performance.**

**For shopping center service industry case example, for this suitation, e.g. shopping center's facilities are enough or are placed to the suitable locations in order to let the shopping center's customers to feel comfortable to shopping when they enter this shopping center as well as whether the shopping center's facilities can influence the customer service staffs to serve whose shopping customers easily or difficult, due to whether the shopping center's facilities whether are adequate supplied or their locations are the best suitable positions to influence their service performance to let them to feel easier or comfortable to serve their customers in any large size shopping centers. For example, whether the lamps' lighting energy is enough to let the shoppers to feel safe to walk to visit any shops when there are many shoppers were walking to cause crowd and they feel diffuclt to walk to avoid any body contact to any one in busy time when the shopping center has no enough lights to let them to see anywhere in the shopping center's dark environment. Then it will influence customer service staffs to feel difficult to find any shopping center customers, e.g. when two shopping center customers are fighting in one location where is far away to the shopping customer service staffs and securities in the shopping center, because the shopping center is large and it has no enough light to let the customer service staffs and securities to find their frighting location to deal their fighing behavior and other shopping center's shoppers will feel very dangerous to walk their fighting location to avoid to close them. Then, it will has possible to cause death or hurt to any one of these two fighting shoppers ,even other shoppers' lifes. Because the shopping center's securities and customer service staffs who need to spend much time to find their fighting location, it will delay they can bring the policemen to their fighting location when they arrive this shopping center's destination in short time in order**

**to solve their fighting behavior to influence all shoppers' lifes in this shopping center. Hence, the shopping center whether it has enough lamps number and the lamps' light whether is enough, these lighting facilities will influence any shopping center customer service staffs and securities who can spend less time to arrive any locations to deal any urgent matters.**

**For another suitation in shopping center, if the shopping center has no enough paying telephone service facilities to supply shoppers to phone to anyone when they feel need to phone to any in the shopping center. Then, it will lead to some shoppers decide to find where the shopping center's receiption's telephone to supply to them to phone call to anyone. If ther are ten shoppers are waiting to use the shopping center's receiption's telephone to phone call to their friend or family within one minute. Thus, it will influence the reception customer service staffs feel difficult to arrange how to distribute the only one telephone to these ten shoppers to use to phone call their friend or family when they are queuing within their one minute waiting time in the shopping center's reception. If these ten shoppers can not use the receiption telephone to phone call anyone. hen, they will feel disatisfactory and complain to the reception service staffs unpolitely. So, lacking enough facilities in the shopping center's any where, it will possible to influence their shopping centers' shoppers to feel all shopping center's service staff individual performance to be poor. It means that if the shopping center expects to improve customer satisfaction to its customer service staff's behavioral performance, it meets have enough facilities to be supplied in the shopping center to let its shoppers to feel it is one comfortable and safe shopping center. In conclusion, shopping center's facilities will have possible to influence shoppers' feeling to evaluate its customer service staffs to evaluate whether their service attitudes are good or poor indirectly.**

- **Can facility management improve productivity**

**The productivity means resources ( input) is therefore the amount of products or services ( output), which is produced by them. Hence, higher ( improved) productivity means that more is produced with the same expectton of resource, i.e. at the same cost is terms of land materials, machine, time or labor. Alternatively, it means same amount is produced at less labor cost in term sof land, material, machine, time for labor that is utilized. So, it brings this question: How can facility management improve productivity? I shall explain as these several aspects, it is possible to be improved productivity from (FM) successfully.**

**Improved productivity of farm land: If the farming land has better facility management to bring advantages by using better seed, better facilities of cultivation and most fertilizer. It is in the agricultural sense is increased ( improved). So, facility management can bring benefits to any land resource to raise productivity in possible. It implies that the productivity of land used for better facility management of industrial purposes is said to have been increased if the output of products or service within that area of industrial land is increased output aim.**

**Improved productivity of material: If the factory has improved better equipment by facility management method to assist skillful workers to raise the manufacture cloth number, then the productivity of the cloth number is improved by (FM) method.**

**Improved productivity of labour: When the factory has good manufacturing equipment facilities to be supplied to improve methods of work to product more producing number per hour, then (FM) improved productivity of worker. Hence, in any workplaces, when organization has good facilities, it will influence employees to raise productivities in possible, because they need often to improved equipment facilties manufacture products to achieve higher producton number aim.**

- ***Can facility management raise bank employee***

  ***productivity***

Bank workplace environment is busy, the bank counter service staffs need to contact many bank clients to help them to serve or withdraw money from bank's counters. Whether does the quality of environment in bank workpace will influence the determination level of employee's motivation, subsequent performance productivity in bank working environment. For example, if the bnk's staffs need work under inconvenient conditions , it will bring low performance and face occupatinal health diseases causing high abenteeism and turnover.

In general, bank size is usually small, it will have many bank clients enter bank to contact counter staffs to need them to help them to save or withdraw money. So, it will bring air pollution the crowd queue in every bank counter challenge when the bank has many people are queue waiting in counters to queue. So, bank working condition problem relates to environmental and physical factors which will influence every bank counter staff individual working performance to serve bank clients satisfactory. However, bank staffs need to deal many documents concern every client personal data every day. So, they need to spend much time to use computer and painting machines. This is particularly true for these employees who spend most of the day operating a computer terminal in bank workplace. As more and more computers are being installed in workplaces, an increasing number of business has been adopting designs for bank offices installment. So, bank needs have effective facilities management design because of demand of bank staffs for more human comfort.

An good equipment facility management for bank staffs to use conveniently, it is assumed that better workplace environment can motives bank employees and produces better productivity. Hence, bank office environment can be described in terms of physical and behavioral components to influence bank staffs to work inefficiently. To achieve high level of abnk employee productivity, bank organizations must ensure that the physical environment in conductive to bank different department organizational needs, facilitating interaction and privacy,

**formality and informality, functionalit and disciplinarily, e.g. house loan or private loan departmets, counter service department, visa card application department.**

**Thus, in a high safe privary facility management working environment will let different department bank staffs feel safe to worry about privacy loss in possible. So, the improving bank facility to bring safe and high privacy to avoid bank client individual loss in working environment issue, the facility management can be results to bring these benefits, such as in a reduction in a number of complaints and absenteeism and an increase in productivity.**

- **Can (FM) create value to organization?**

**(FM) can reduce managing facilties as a strategic resource to add value to the organization and its overall performance, e.g. saving the energy in building and take care of shuttle buses and parking facilities space management for brikes, on economic efficiency and effectiveness, or good price and value for the organization.**

**If the organization expects to apply (FM) process to save energy, it depends on possible input factors, i.e. interventions in the accommodation facilities services. So, it seems that the organization expects to save its energy consumption in its building. It needs have goos space management facilities between parking its shuttle buses and brikes in its property's car park.**

**Why does space facility management is important to influence efficiency and productivity. For one school's building example, when the school decides none of the two gymnasiums student sport entertainment centers to be built in order to reduce financial cost and higher benefits. Remarkably, the use of space with the school overall strategic goals , such as creating spaces that better can support the teaching, motivate students and teachers, attract more students and increase the utilisation of existing space to accomodate an increasing number of students.**

**If it hopes to make high quality teaching facilities on student's choice where to study. The school will need to choose to build either one comfortable and new design facility teaching accommodation or build two gymnasium sport entertainment centers in its limited land space either for students' learning or sport aim. Due to it feels new teaching accommodcation can make more attractive to increase students numbers to choose it to study more than building two new gymnasusm sport centers to let them do sport in school.**

**Hence, space choise (FC) management strategy will be one important considerable issue, when the organization has limited land space resources to make choose to build any constructions in order to increase many clients number. Such as the school organization has limited stortage land resource to let it to build either two gymnasium sport entertainment centers or one new teaching accommodation in order to attract many students to choose it to learn. Hence, it needs to gather data to make more accurate evaluation to decide how to apply its space facility to choose to build these both kinds of buildings in order to achieve the attractive student learning choice aim, so whether teh two sport entertainment activity centers or one new teaching accommodation choice, it needs to gater information to decide whether the school ought to choose to build which kind of building in order to achieve the increase of student number aim, so space facility management will be this school's land shortage problem.**

**The relationship between facility management and consumer behavior**

**How and why shop facility management can influence consumer individual shopping behavior? If it is possible, what shop facility management factors can influence their consumption decision when they enter the shop to plan to buy anything. I shall indicate some shop case studied to expline whether how and why every shop's facility management can influence consumer individual consumption desire when any one**

**consumer enters any shops.**

- **Shop's low ceiling height location (FM) influcence consumer behavior**

**Can the shop's ceiling height influence shoppers' shopping behavior? Can the shops's variation in ceiling height can influence how consumers process information to decide to make purchase decision in the shops, e.g. for this suitation, when the consumer enters the shop, he/she feels the ceiling height is low and it has a lamp wil contact his/her head in possible. So, he/she chooses to move far away from the low ceiling beight location in the shop. It is possible that shop's ceiling low height and the lamp locates at the ceiling low height position will influence many customers' choices to leave the low ceiling height and lamp location, then the shop's low ceiling height will have possible to influenced many customers to choose to find the another shop to buy the similar kind of products , due to the lamp locates in the low ceiling height, so this lamp and low ceiling height will be possible factor to influence any shoppers who won't choose to walk to this dangerous location in the shop. If the shop's all spaces are ceiling height and it has many lamps are located at the low ceiling height spaces. Then, it will be serious to cause many shoppers do not want to spend too much time to choose any products in the shop because they feel dangerous to walk to the any low ceiling height lamps' locations in the shop.**

**Hence, hoe to design the different concept may be activated by the showroom ceiling if it were relatively high, as it tends to be in mall stores, versus low, as it is in most strip mall shops and outlet centers. Relatively high ceilings may bring safe shopping emotion to let any consumers to feel thoughts related to freedom, whereas lower ceilings may let consumers to feel dangerous to walk the locations in any shops. Hence it seems any shops ought not neglect whether their ceiling height is tall and the lamps ought avoid to locate in any low ceiling height locations in order to influence**

**consumers number to be decreased.**

- **Can house facility management influence consumer individual purchase intention?**

**When one new property is built, whether the property consumers will consider how the new property is facilited to influence their purchase intention to the property will the new property's (FM) influence buyers in real estate markets' preferences choice and living interest. Any new property's internal characteristics of the house unit itsel , such as rooms available, when example, of external are location, accessibility to utilities services and facilities will have possible to influence the property buyer's final property purchase decision, so it seems that even the property price is cheap, it is not represent the property buyer will choose to buy the property, if he/she feels the property's facility mangement is poorer to compare other similar kinds of properties.**

**So, it can help real estate analysts better explain and predict the behavior of decision makers in real estate markets. Property consumers will search for property information, concerns the property's quality, price distinctiveness, ability, facility mangement, service of the property's external environment to decide whether the property is high value to choose to buy to compare other kinds of properties.**

**However, the external environmental forces, such as limited resources, e.g. time or financial will influence whose property consumption choice and living the property's satisfaction feeling ( represent) a feedback machanism from post-property purchase reflection used to inform subsequent decisions. The process of the property buyer's leaving experience will serve to influence the extent to which the property consumer how to consider future next time property purchases decision and new information methods. Hence, when one property consumer chooses to buy a house, it refers house features ar house internal attributes , such**

as quality of building, the design as well as internal and external design, which are important factors for a property consumer when he/she needs to select and purchases one house.

The other (FM) factors which can influence the property consumers' needs, include living space as features, such as the size of kitchen, bathroom, bedroom, living bath and other rooms available in the house. The environment of housing area is also important factor, e.g. the condition of the neighbourhood, attractiveness of the area, quality of neighbouring houses, type of neighbouring houses, type of neighbouring houses, density of housing, wooded area or free coverage, slope of the attractive views, open space, non-residential uses in the areas vacant sites, traffic noise, level of owner-occupation in neighbourhoos, level of education in neighbourhood level of income in neighbourhood, security from crime, quality of schools, religious of neighbourhood, transportation , shopping center, sport entertainment can be supplied to close to the house area. All these human related issue of the property's location will also influence the property buyer's living location selection. Hence, above (FM) influence property consumer purchase behavior, it is based on the relationship behavior. The consumer's house purchase intention and house features, living space, environment and distance to recreation center, supermarket, library etc. public facilities variable (FM) factors.

In conclusion, the house internal space facility management and external environment facility management factors will influence property consumer individual house purchase intention.

- **The effects of in-store shelf design facility management factor influences consumer behavior**

Can every store retailer's shelf design influence supermarket and large retail stores shoppers' behaviors when they visit the stores? However, currently many stores tend to build on

**traditional and repetitive design for their store shelf layout, it brings results in outdated store layouts.**

**Another important store shelf layout design aspect, retailer should consider carefully is the allocation of products on shelves. So, it seems that efficienct shelf space allocation management does not only minimize the economic threats of empty product shelves, it can also lead to higher consumer satisfaction, a better customer relationship.**

**Why does supermarket shelves design is important? Any retail tore will sell product category within a shelf. They can use the same nominal category , e.g. negular crisps next to light crisps, same food prouct shelf. Anyway, a goal-based shelf display can contain several product, that determine a common consumer goal, e.g. fair trade. Hence, these two categorical product structuring methods are also described in terms of how to put product, or food on shelf benefit and attribute -based product categories.**

**These shelf design food or product storing method will have more influence consumers to choose to buy the supermarket or retail store food or products more easily , due to products, or food put on their shelf very convenient and systematic to attract consumers' shopping consideration to the supemarket or retail store.**

- **Music (FM) environment influence consumer consumption desire**

**Is it possible that shop music (FM) environment can raise consumer purchase desire? In one shop or supermarket, it can provide soft music (FM) equipment to let consumers can listen soft music or songs in the supermarket or retail shop when the are staying to spend more time shopping and whether soft music facility can be expected to raise customer individual value-added options to the music facility shop in the supermarket ot retail shop.**

**Can the music facilities prolong consumers to stay in the store? It is possible that tempo soft music can influence consumers to stay longer time in restaurants and supermarkets and retail shops. It is possible that the different types of music (FM) in any supemarket, restaurant, retail shop owning music listening facility shopping environment. It will have possible to influence consumers to prolong staying in their shops. For example, one wine selling retail shop has classical music (FM) listening equipment to let consumers to listen when they enter the wine shop, it is possible to cause consumers to choose to buy more expensive wine products. Some researchers indicate when the wine shop owns classical music facility to let all consumers can list classical music when they walk in the wine ship, it can evoke the wine consumers to choose to buy purchasing higher prices wine products in the long term classical music listening environment. Otherwise, in a fitness sport center, musical fir and excite or popular music ( FM) environment can attract fitness sport players' emotion to play and kind of fitness sport facility longer time. Also, in one supermarket, the soft music facilities listening environment can persuade or attract food consumers to spend more time in the mall consuming food or beverage also purchase othe products more easily, due to they will listen soft music to be influenced to choose to prolong staying time in the supermarket. It seems that it has relationship between retail shop's music facility environment and consumer's emotion will be influenced by these different kinds of soft music or songs to raise consumption desire in the supermarket, if some consumers like to proplong to stay longer consuming time in the owning music facility environment's retail shop.**

**In fact, some researchers indicate the owning background music facility selling environment's ship , it can affect consumer decision making, memory, concentration consumption desire. So, classical , jazz soft music facility ought be installed in restaurants, retail shops, restaurants' environment. Otherwise, popular , exciting, noise, pop music facilty ought be installed in fitness**

sport centers, theme park entertainment parks business places in order to influence fitness sport players or theme park entertainers to prolong playing or entertaining time to feel real sport or entertainment theme park playing machine facility's entertainment enjoyable feeling as well as attracting restaurant or supermarket or retail shop's consumers to proplong their staying time to make consumption decisions. Hence, it seems that music facility environment can raise consumers' consumption desire in possible.

- University bookstore atmospheric factors how to influence student's purchase book behavior?

Any university bookstore how to do international control and structuring of book internal environment to raise students' purchase book desires in university itself school's bookstore, it will be one popular question to any universities. Hence, whether the university bookstore internal (FM) factors include: lighting, music, colors, scents, temperature, layout and general cleanliness as well as university external factors include: the university bookstore shape/size, windows, university parking facility for students availability and location,which can play an influential role of the university bookstore image in order to influence the university itself students to choose to buy books from themselves bookstore or university outside bookstores.

Whether the university student needs to spend how long individual learning time and how mcuh learning nervous to spend time to choose any kinds of book in the univeristy bookstore or outside bookstores, this issue , he/she will consider. Because he/she does want to expect spend much time and nervous to choose to buy books in any bookstore. If the universitt's bookstore physical location and internal (FM) desing image can let its target student customers to feel it's all book products are stored in any attractive internal book shelves places, e.g. the cheapest and the most expensive different subjects of text books

**are stored in one system method to bring the positive image of value snd quality in order to let university target student customers can find their books' choice location to spend less time to search any books to read in the unviersity bookstore easily.**

**However, due to learning time is shortage to every university student of the universty's book shelves can display all text books in the attractive right locations in the university bookstore as well as the university's bookstore ought has an adequate space to let university students to walk to anywhere and find any subjects of text books and compare their book sale prices in the bookstore's any shelves' locations easily when they walk to the subject of book shelf location, then they can make accurate decision either to buy the right kind of subject book or not buy it to read in the short time. They will ferl their book choice purchase decision making process won't influence their learning time in themselves univeristy. Then, the university students will be influenced by themselve university's bookstore's attractive external university facilites in the univeristy's any teaching places and the university's bookstore internal attractive environment facility image which can influence the students to make final choices to buy their liking books to read from their university's itself bookstore. Hence, the university's bookstore internal and external building environment (FM) design factors will influence its students whether choose to buy from themselves bookstore or another outside general bookstore.**

- **How and why does retail atmospheric environment influence consumers behavior in retail shop?**

**Any shop's internal facility management design can influence atmospheric environment to influence consumer individual shopping desire, e.g. colour, lighting, music, crowding, design and layout factors, which internal shop (FM) environment can influence the first time shopping visiting client ' cognitive process how to feel the shop store image. Such as if the store's (FM)**

environment can bring enjoyable and fun and happy image to let them to feel shopping's enjoyment.

In conclusion, when consumers will like to stay longer time in the store. Due to the store's internal (FM) atmospheric environment can attract them to stay longer time in the store. Then, the customer's shopping value will raise and it can bring purchasing intention and shopping satisfaction. How can (FM) influence retail atmospheric physical (FM) environment ? Can (FM) bring indirect relationship to influence how the consumer individual causes positive or negative purchase intention when he/she has influence to proplong staying desire in the store, when the shop has good (FM) , it will bring long time to make consumption chance in the shop.

Facility management brings what benefits to entertainment theme parks

In entertainment theme park organizations, they must need to have different kinds of leisure playing machine facilities to supply to visitors to choose to play. So, facility management (FM) must need to imrpove any one entertainment theme parkj machine facility quality, it aims to avoid accidents occur , due to any leisure machine facilities are old or damage when they are used to operate in daily long opening time. Hence, FM must be needed to improve any entertainment theme parks' different kinds of leisure playing machine equipment frequently. If any one theme park leisure machine facility has poor FM in order to improve its machine quality. Consequently, this kind of leisure theme park leisure playing mahcine may be sudden to bring accidents occur, when any one visitor chooses this one of leisure playing machine facility to play. It may cause the player to hurt, even die in possible. Hence, FM to any entertainment theme park playing machine equipment , it may be one major facility repair management srtategy to any entertainment theme parks leisure playing machine facilities, because any one leisure playing machine facilities may bring any one visiot body hurt when the playing machine is old. Instead of FM can bring safety and playinf machine facilities quality

**improvement benefits to any one entertainment theme park leisure playing machine, whether FM to entertainment theme parks can bring psotive playing of leisure emotion to any one theme park visitor. I shall attempt to discuss as below:**

**Firstly, we need to know that any kinds of entertainment theme parks why they need to implement FM strategy. Why FM can bring advantages to any kinds of entertainment theme parks. In fact, the benefits of facility management to entertainment theme parks, it enables a more cost-effective working process within any kinds of the theme park any leisure playing machine facilities, such as theme park leisure playing sevice business. It improves the efficiency and it can help the theme park to manage health and safety requirements in accordance with industry regulations. It increases lifespan of a theme park any kinds of leisure playing machines, they are the theme park fixed assets, such as theme park's any kinds of leisure playing machine facilities. New theme parks and attractions can also improve the image of a destination increase tourism and hence economic benefits for the local community , and provide education and entertainment opportunities to the public.**

**Hence, it is common sense, if the theme park can have good FM to improve its any leisure playing facilities in order to avoid any accident occurrence , when any one visitor chooses to play its any one lesiure machine. Then, it can bring positive safe emotion feeling to satisfy any one visitor whose individual playing safe need to any kinds of playing leisure machines. I believe that its visitors number will not decrease, even increases significantly forever. Hence , the major roles of a theme park facility manager, is that to ensure the upkeep and manintenance of its any one entertainment playing machines, e.g. rolling rides, water rides etc. So, that they meet both safety and health standards to let any one visitors to feel safe to play.**

**In fact, the scope of facilities management covers two main areas: space and infrastructure , such as planning, design and workplace, construction, occupancy , maintenance and furniture**

as well as people and organization ( such as catering, cleaning and HR, hospitality, accounting and marketing efficient operation in office ) both aspects. Hence, these are 6 main facilities to ensure one available for any familiry theme plars. For leisure theme park case, rides and attractions are needed for all ages of any one theme park visitors. This is perhaps the most imprtant, as different parks will have different target audiences, e.g. refreshments, shops, toilets, and parking , access facilities and any one kind of leisure playing machines, such as rolling rides, water rides etc.

Hence, a theme park is a type of amusement park that bases its choice of which kinds of leisure playing facility structures and attractions around a central theme often featureing multiple areas with different themes. Unlike temporary and mobile fun fairs and carnivals, amusement parks are stationary and built for long lasting operation. Hence, every theme park must need have a photogenic, iconic landmark that draws people into the park, beautiful landscaping , enough available attraction capacity to keep peak waits for non-new attractions under 90 minutes, all of these are other faciliities. They must also need to manage to keep more attraction to theme park any one visitor to feel enjoyable and comfortable to play any one theme park leisure playing machines.

What advantages to the theme park implements FM strategy? For Ocean Park example, it aims to let visitors feel themed ocean animal recreational and educational and leisure park experience. So, it must need to upgrade to improve its any facilities to avoid long time repaire spending expenditure. FM project may include: modifying sections of ocean park road, which is a local distributor, around the existing bus terminus , drain works, tunneling and geotechnical works, bulk excavation and slope works, site clearance, modification to bus terminus, taxi stands as well as utilities works including power supply distribution, electrical substations, freshwater and saltwater reservoirs, water supply distribution, gas supply distribution, telecommunications networks, landscope irrigation network to the ocean park any one

**ocean fish reservoirs, primary life support system works for animal keeping, area development works include elevated walkways, external lighting, external escalators, bridges, parkwide systems works include: signage, background, music system, toilet facilities, guard sheds, first and facilities, communication systems , CCTV systems and waste facilities, landscape or theming works, themed concern pavements, hardscape soft landscaping, water and rockwork features, visual intrusion screens, area props and artwork etc. works for the attractions venues include: animal exhibits, marine animal, terrestrial animal, aviaries , bind exhibits, individual life support systems for animal , exhibits and non- animal related attractions, e.g. shipwreck play area, bamboo maze etc. installation of rides interactive rides , transportation rides etc. , works for venues include : event halls, outdoor live show area, cinema band stands, work for the merchandise / retail facilities include souvonir stores, novelty stores, games ascade, photo shops etc. in the ocean park.**

**Moreover, any ocean park also have works for the food and baverage facilities include: restaurants, ballery, food casrts as well as back of house facilities include: ocean park offices, break areas, warehouses , centralized facilities, operational facilities etc. , even the ocean park inside hotel development facilities. All of these may bring positive or negative leisure activities impacts to influence any one of this ocean park visitor individual emotion significantly, if he /she feel comfortable and enjoyable , when they enter this ocean park. This ocean park whole natural environment may influence they like to stay long time in this ocean park. So, when they can stay long time in this ocean park, they may spend money to live hotels, spend money to play any leisure machines and spend time to go to shopping, or buying tickets to see any movies in this ocean park. All of this ocean park natural environment facilities and leisure playing machines improvement may influence any one visitor individual emotion either negative or positive feeling.**

On conclusion, any theme parks must need to implement FM strategy to improve their theme parks inside natural environment and leisure playing machines quality and hotel living facilities and theme park external transport tool stations facilities, e.g. taxi, bus , railway station distance to convenience any one visitor can catch any one kind of public transport tool to arrive this theme park in short time easily. Also, any theme parks need to impove environment facilities in order to let any one visitor feels comfortable and enhoyable feeling when they choose this theme park to play. Consequently, the theme park's visitors number may be influenced to increase by their positive playing emotion feeling.

Facility management brings what advantages to theatres

Theatre performance needs performers own proficient performance skills to perform their music, or art performances to let audiences feel happy and satisfactory to see or listen their performances in the theatre hall, instead of performers their individual performing factor. Facility management (FM) in the theatre any facilities, e.g. performing hall, toilets, seats, theatre cater restaurants, car parking location etc. different theatre inside and outside facilities may also influence any one theatre audience whether he / she can feel enjoyable to see or listen any one art or music perfofmance, because if they feel the theatre facilities are poor quality. This theatre poor facilities feeling factor may also influence they expect to go to this theatre to see any art performances or listen any music performance again. Hence, instead of theatre performancers their individual performance skillful factor, any theatres their whole theatre inside and outside facilities will may also influence any one theatre music or art audience to choose to buy ticket to enter this theatre to see or listen any performances again. So, any one theatre facilities satisfactory feeling may also be another important factor to influence the theatre performance tickets sale number. I shall attempt to indicate the different kinds of facilities aspects, that any one theatre ought need to considerate their facilities improvement aspects issue as below:

Firstly, we need to know whether what theatre essential facilities elements may be. Then, I shall discuss how to manage theatre facilities in orde to improve its performance to assist any one performance to raise their performance level and bring more listening music or seeing art performance satisfactory and comfortable feeling to every theatre audience, when they are sitting one to two hours, even more than two hours in the theatre/

Hence, whole theatre inside facilities may influence any one audience individual satisfactory feeling, instead of seeing the art performers or listening the music performers their performances in the theatre halls. Although any one theatre audience makes decision to buy the ticket that their aims is general listening the music performance or seeing the art performance., but when they must need to sit long time in the theatre seats to enjoy any performances in the theatre, the extra ( another) theatre facilities factor may also influence their satisfacgory feeling, e.g. if the theatre performance is music performance, all audience feel the theatre sound system facilities are poor to influence their listening music performance satisfactory feeling, e.g. more noise or feeling difficulty to listen soft music from the performers. Then, the whole music performance quality will be influenced to worse listening standard leve, it is not due to the music performer individual music playing skillful aspect, it is possible due to the theatre whole music sound system facilities or music sound equipment can not achieve the actural music sound satisfactory listening performance standard level effect to let any one music audience feels difficulty to listen the music performers how play their music performance proficiently.

So, it seems that theatre music sound system facilities may influence any one music performance standard level to be worse to the whole music poor performance process. It is not possible to any one music performance individual music playing skills whether he can play proficient music sound system facilities to improve or repair frequently to cause the whole music

**performance quality level to become worse indirectly. Hence, theatre music sound system facilities which may influence whole music performance level either to raise or reduce indiirectly.**

**Any theatre needs to be created the facility and workflow management module to coordinate events, perople and resources across organization;s available venues in order to pull down from and create information in the theatre database to manage theatre venue, staff and audiences. Because covid 19 disease occurs, it influences many theatres need to keep clean seating environment to avoid any one owning covid 19 disease audience enters the theatre easily. So, the theatre cleaning seating managing method and crowd controlling quese method both aim to avoid covid 19 disease occurrence in the theatre,. when any one theatre staff or audience enter the theatre. So, any theatre cleaning and safe FM must be raise improvement level.**

**The theatre FM seating managing needs to conside: The occuring in different venues, the theatre resources needed at each location at a particular time, theatre staff memebers needed at diffeent locations or times, e.g. which events are occurring in each venue, the theatre resources needed at each location at a location, tasks requiring completion from quick 1- perspon to do items to entire operations involving several people like set construction or rehearsal before any performances began in the theatre, an ordering of tasks and dependence on each other , ie parinting can not begin until construction is completed and grouping of similar items together.**

**Hence, when the theatre can orgainze one effective FM strategy , it may help the theatre organization and art/music performance organization to arrange those tasks efficiently, such as scheduling: people ( theatre staffs, performaners, theatre places, e.g. venues , theatre resources / supplies , e.g. every art/ music performance project), distribution ( calendars can be updated internally before whole month all theatres performances begin in order to any performance time can be viewed on the theatre internet ), billing ( creating a quote and administration tasks). So, theatre daily taskj**

**list, meeting scheduling, with staffs email notification etc. theatre administration tasks can be influenced to raise efficience when the theatre can have effective FM strategy.**

**In general, theatre is one music / art performance venue ( place). It may include: theatre venue, space management, building maintenance, testing and inspection management , such as covid 19 disease is for every theatre audience before they can permit to enter the theatre as well as theatre staffs, performers and audience body contact management in the theatre hall inside any environment that they can stay long time in the clean theatre environment. SO, effective anf efficient organized to any one performance, theatre FM ought need to keep any one whole performance process in safe and clean working environment, e.g. theatre task facilities are safe, and theatre audiences and theatre staffs and performers , they can contact in safe and clean crowd theatre environment often.**

**In fact, Fm in theatre , it uses specialized theatre knowledge to provide technical direction and control over all theatre systems, including sound, lighting, projections, riugging, counterweight system, and front of house procedures involved with productions with an emphasis on safety. Hence, FM in theatrical environment is the definition of four core values. They may include: responsibility means to guarantee all the theatre installations to be in perfect condition and work properly every simgle day; flexibility means to work day and nught to finish maintenance work before the theatre audiences arrive for another daily performance, passion means to deliver the best theatre experience for the theatre audiences controlling all elements in services, ambitions means besides showing the best musical shows on stage in one of the beautiful theatres. So, FM intheatre may include: security, climate contol, cleaning, mechancial, music sound system management, engineering, electronics, reception system management, mail, fire protection, lighting, maintenance, rehearsal performance facility arrangement etc. for the theatre performance before and after service in order to achieve the**

**saisfactory performance to let auiences to feel.**

**On conclusion, any nowadays theatre organizations must need have effective and efficient facility management (FM) stategy in order to let audiences to feel safe and confident and comfortable feeling when they are sitting down in the seats to spend long time to listen or see any kinds of art or music performances in the theatre hall. So, when they feel the theatre can provide comfortable and safe and clean inside theater hall environment to see or listen any art or music performances. Consequently, the theatre ticket sale number may be influenced to raise in possible. So, I can explain why any theatres ought need FM to assist themselves theatre operation.**

9 798887 725406

Printed by Libri Plureos GmbH in Hamburg,
Germany